Mark Twain
at Work!

written by
Howard Goldsmith

illustrated by
Frank Habbas

Aladdin
New York London Toronto Sydney Singapore

To Frona, with love—H. G.
For Ginny and Amy—F. H.

First Aladdin edition June 2003

ALADDIN PAPERBACKS
An imprint of Simon & Schuster Children's Publishing Division
1230 Avenue of the Americas
New York, NY 10020

Book design by Lisa Vega
The text of this book was set in Century Old Style.

Printed in the United States of America
4 6 8 10 9 7 5

Library of Congress Cataloging-in-Publication Data

Goldsmith, Howard.
Mark Twain at work! / by Howard Goldsmith : illustrated
by Frank Habbas.
p. cm.—(Ready-to-read childhood of the famous Americans)
Summary: A beginning biography of Mark Twain that relates the childhood
incident which grew into one of his most famous books: The Adventures of
Tom Sawyer.
ISBN 978-0-689-85399-8 (Aladdin pbk.) — ISBN 978-0-689-85400-2 (Aladdin Library edition)
0212
1. Twain, Mark, 1835–1910—Childhood and youth—Juvenile literature.
2. Authors, American—19th century—Biography—Juvenile literature.
[1. Twain, Mark, 1835–1910—Childhood and youth. 2. Authors, American.]
I. Habbas, Frank, ill. II. Title. III. Series.
PS1332 .G65 2003
818'.409—dc21

2002006148

Mark Twain was born
in a small Missouri town
in 1835.

His real name was Samuel Clemens.
Young Sam and his cousins
were close friends.
They played together a lot.

They loved to explore the woods,
climb trees, pick berries,
and swim in the brook.

Sam never liked to sit still
for too long.
His mother once asked,
"Sam, do you carry
jumping beans in your pockets?"
"No," Sam answered. "Why?"

"Because you are always
hopping about
like a jumping bean."

For Sam,

school hours seemed too long.

One day he decided

to have some fun.

He put a garter snake in his pocket
and brought it to school.
"Look, everyone!" Sam called,
dangling the snake.

"Eeeeeek!" his classmates screamed,
jumping up on their seats.
"A snake!"

The snake wriggled its way
across the room.
It stopped at the feet
of their teacher, Mr. Cross.

Mr. Cross glared across the room
at Sam.

"Sam-u-el Lang-horne Clem-ens!"
he called.

"Take that snake outside! At once!"

"Yes, sir," Sam said,
scooping up the snake.

The next day Mr. Cross

spoke to Sam's mother

about the snake.

"I am sorry," Sam said,

looking down at his shoes.

Sam's mother punished him
by making him paint
the tall, wide fence
around their yard.

"That's an awful lot of work!"

Sam complained,

staring at the fence.

It looked a mile high.

"Blame yourself!" his mother answered.

Sam asked his friend Sandy
to help him paint the fence.
"I am sorry, Sam," Sandy said.
"I have to go fetch water
from the well. Bye!"

"Oh no!" Sam said to himself.

"Now what will I do?"

In answer to his prayers,

along came Sam's friend Will Bowen.

"That's an awful lot of work!"
Will said.

"Work?" Sam answered.

"It's fun! Can't you see that?"

"Fun?" Will said, puzzled.

Sam swept paint back and forth
across the fence, over and over.

"Nothing is work

if you enjoy doing it," Sam said.

"Can I brush awhile?"

Will asked.

"What will you give me to brush?" Sam said.

"Give you?" Will asked, puzzled.

"Of course," Sam said.

"Nothing for nothing."

"Okay," Will said.

He gave Sam his apple.

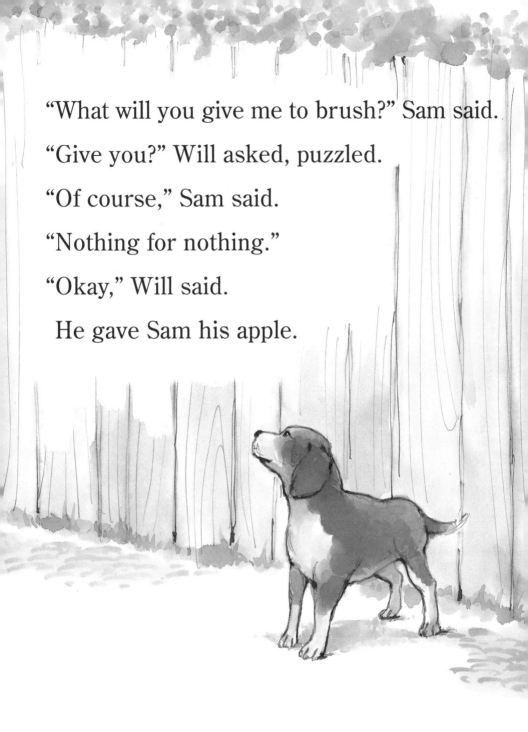

Sam chewed the apple
as he watched Will paint.
Soon John Briggs came along.
John gave Sam a tadpole
to let him swing the brush.

When John got tired,
Sam traded the next chance
to brush
to his friend Frank.

By late afternoon
all the boys in town
had painted the fence.
Sam was not tired at all!

Plus he now had two tadpoles,

ten marbles, a box of worms,

five pieces of orange peel,

and other things.

Someday, Sam promised himself,
I am going to write all this down.
He would turn it into a funny story.
He loved making people laugh.

As he grew older
he learned to weave
webs of magic words
that cast a spell.

Years later Sam wrote books
under the name Mark Twain.
The story of the fence
grew into one of Mark Twain's
most famous books:
The Adventures of Tom Sawyer.

Mark Twain became one of America's favorite humorists.

After *The Adventures of Tom Sawyer,*
Mark Twain wrote *The Adventures of Huckleberry Finn.*
He said most of those adventures were true.
They all happened when he was a boy.

Here is a timeline of Mark Twain's life:

1835   Born in Florida, Missouri, as Samuel Langhorne Clemens

1839   Clemens family moves to Hannibal, Missouri

1843   Twain attends William Cross's one-room schoolhouse.
Young Twain writes:

> "Cross by name and cross by nature—
> Cross jumped over an Irish potato."

1848   Apprentices at the Missouri *Courier*

1852   Twain's first published sketch appears in the *Boston Carpet Bag*

1857   Begins work as an apprentice pilot on the Mississippi River

1861   Moves to Nevada with his brother Orion and tries mining

1862   Takes a job as a reporter, for the Virginia City *Territorial Enterprise*

1865   Wins fame with his comic tale, "Jim Smiley and his Jumping Frog" (later published as "The Celebrated Jumping Frog of Calaveras County")

1866   Gives his first lecture on his experiences, beginning a career as a humorous lecturer

1870   Marries Olivia Langdon

1871   They settle in Hartford, Connecticut

1876   *The Adventures of Tom Sawyer* is a great success

1882   Publishes *The Prince and the Pauper*

1884   *The Adventures of Huckleberry Finn* is published in London; comes out the following year in America

1889   Publishes *A Connecticut Yankee in King Arthur's Court*

1904   Wife Olivia dies at age sixty

1910   Dies at age seventy-five in Redding, Connecticut